THE LITTLE BOOK OF PAINFULLY AWFUL
DAD JOKES

THINKS YOU
MUST LAUGH
OUT OF RESPECT

How do you organize a space party?
You planet

Why did the scarecrow win an award?
Because he was outstanding in his field.

I only know 25 letters of the alphabet.
I don't know y.

What do you call a factory that makes good products
A satisfactory.

Why did the bicycle fall over?
Because it was two-tired.

DAUGHTER PRACTICING STOICISM

What do you call fake lettuce?
A shamrock.

How do you catch a squirrel?
Climb a tree and act like a nut!

**Did you hear about the math teacher
who's afraid of negative numbers?**
He'll stop at nothing to avoid them.

Why don't oysters donate to charity?
Because they are shellfish.

What do you call a pile of cats?
A meowtain.

DOG IS
FORCED
TO LAUGH
FOR
FOOD!

RIP boiling water,
you will be mist

I once wrote a song about a tortilla,
but it's more of a wrap

A witch's vehicle goes
brrroom brrroom!

The wedding was so beautiful,
even the cake was in tiers

I'm afraid of speed bumps,
but I am slowly getting over it

POOR SON IN PURE DISBELIEVE

Humpty Dumpty had a great fall.
Summer wasn´t too bad either

Why did the whale blush?
Because he saw the ocean´s bottom.

What did the grape say when it got stepped on?
Nothing, it just let out a little wine.

Why don‘t eggs tell each other secrets?
Because they might crack up.

Why don‘t seagulls fly over the bay?
Because then they‘d be bagels.

CAUGHT?!!
DAD'S HIDING JOKE BOOK IN CAR MAINTEANCE MAGAZINE!

Did you hear about the guy who invented the knock-knock joke?
He won the ‚no-bell‘ prize

I‘ve got a great joke about construction,
but I‘m still working on it

What do you get from a pampered cow?
Spoiled milk

What do you call a lazy baby kangaroo?
A pouch potato!

What‘s a robot‘s favorite snack?
Computer chips

DAUGHTER IN AWE
WHEN SHE DISCOVERS SHE
CAN JUST COVER HER EARS

How does a penguin build its house?
Igloos it together.

Why did the tomato turn red?
Because it saw the salad dressing!

How do celebrities keep cool?
They have many fans

Did you hear about the claustrophobic astronaut?
He just needed a little space.

Why did the golfer bring two pairs of pants?
In case he got a hole in one.

OVER-EXCITED
FATHER
BEFORE TELLING
HIS NEW
DAD JOKE

I once got fired from a canned juice company.
Apparently I couldn't concentrate

I used to play piano by ear.
Now I use my hands

Have you ever tried to catch a fog?
I tried yesterday but I mist

I made a pencil with two erasers.
It was pointless

I'm reading a book about anti-gravity.
It's impossible to put down!

DAD WITH A YOUNG INNOCENT JOKE VICTIM

What has more letters than the alphabet?
The post office!

What do you call a poor Santa Claus?
St. Nickel-less

I asked my dog what's two minus two.
He said nothing.

I don't trust stairs.
They're always up to something

**What does a lemon say
when it answers the phone?**
Yellow!

JOKE TRAUMATIZED DAUGHTER

Why did the coffee file a police report?
It got mugged.

What's a vampire's favorite fruit?
A blood orange.

**What did the janitor say when he
jumped out of the closet?**
Supplies!

Did you hear about the guy who invented Lifesavers?
He made a mint.

Why did the cowboy adopt a wiener dog?
He wanted to get a long little doggie

LET THERE BE BRAIN

How do you make a tissue dance?
You put a little boogie in it.

What did one ocean say to the other ocean?
Nothing, they just waved.

Why did the computer go to therapy?
It had too many bytes of emotional baggage.

What do you call a snowman with a six-pack?
An abdominal snowman.

Why did the chicken join a band?
Because it had the drumsticks.

MEAN LAUGHING DAD
BECAUSE HE KNOWS
YOU CAN´T FLEE FROM
HIS JOKES

Why don't skeletons fight each other?
They don't have the guts.

Did you hear about the cheese factory explosion?
There was nothing left but de-brie.

What did one hat say to the other?
Stay here, I'm going on ahead.

Why don't scientists trust atoms?
Because they make up everything.

What do you call fake spaghetti?
An impasta.

THINKS HE IS PUNNY
WITHOUT
BEER

I used to be addicted to soap,
but I'm clean now.

Spring is here!
I got so excited I wet my plants!

What does a baby computer call his father?
Data.

Why can't a leopard hide?
Because he's always spotted

What do you call an illegally parked frog?
Toad

DAD
WAS A
GOOD
ONE

My dad told me a joke about boxing.
I guess I missed the punch line

What kind of shoes do ninjas wear?
Sneakers!

I ordered a chicken and an egg from Amazon.
I'll let you know...

Shout out to my fingers.
I can count on all of them

What country's capital is growing the fastest?
Ireland. Every day it's Dublin

TIP!
TELL YOUR DAD JOKES -
THIS WILL MAKE HIM TIRED
AND YOU CAN BRING HIM
TO BED WAY EARLIER!!!

Why are spiders so smart?
They can find everything on the web

Did you hear about the circus fire?
It was in tents

Can February March?
No, but April May!

Wanna hear a joke about paper?
Never mind—it's tearable.

I could tell a joke about pizza,
but it's a little cheesy

GUILTY!!

What is a funny mountain called?
Hill-arious

I used to hate facial hair,
but it grew on me.

Some people think prison is one word,
but to robbers, it's the whole sentence.

I poured root beer in a square glass.
Now I just have beer.

I had a dream about being a muffler.
I woke up exhausted.

PUNNY GRANDPA
ALERT
DEFCON 2

What kind of music scares balloons?
Pop music

What did the grape say when it got stepped on?
Nothing, it just let out a little wine

What do you call a fish wearing a crown?
A kingfish

How do you get an astronaut's baby to stop crying?
You rocket

How do you make holy water?
You boil the hell out of it

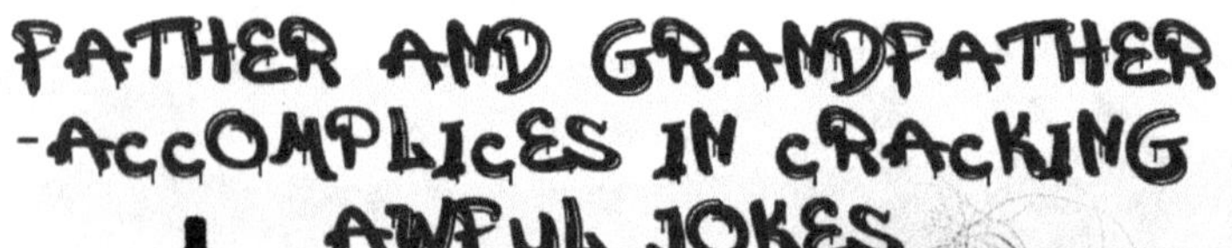

FATHER AND GRANDFATHER
-ACCOMPLICES IN CRACKING
AWFUL JOKES

Did you hear about the fire at the shoe factory?
Unfortunately, many soles were lost

What kind of fish knows how to do an appendectomy?
A Sturgeon

How do you hire a horse?
Put up a ladder

Why did the pony ask for a glass of water?
Because it was a little horse

Why shouldn´t you trust trees?
They seem shady!

NEVER LET
YOUR DAD TELL JOKES
AT DINNER.
THERE WILL BE
DESTRUCTION!

I went to get camouflage pants.
I couldn´t find any.

Did you hear about the guy who afraid of hurdles?
He got over it.

Why did the computer catch cold?
It left a window open

What did the earthquake say when it was done?
Sorry, my fault!

What do lawyers wear to work?
Law suits!

THIS IS
TORTURE

What did one wall say to the other?
I`ll meet you at the corner

What did the zero say to the eight?
That belt looks good on you

Did you hear about the man who cut off his left leg?
He's all right now

What did Baby Corn say to Mama Corn?
Where's Pop Corn?

What's the best thing about Switzerland?
I don`t know, but the flag is a big plus.

DISILLUSIONED DESCENDANTS

What sits on the seabed and has anxiety?
A nervous wreck.

Why is Peter Pan always flying?
He neverlands

What's the best air to breathe if you want to be rich?
Millionaire

Why did the girl toss a clock out the window?
She wanted to see time fly

When two vegans get in an argument,
is it still called a beef?

HARMLESS LOOKING FATHER
TO LULL YOU INTO SAFETY
BEFORE CRACKING
HIS JOKES

What did one plate say to another plate?
Tonight, dinner's on me.

Did you hear about the king that went to the dentist?
He needed to get crowns.

What happens when doctors get frustrated?
They lose their patients.

What do you call a bear with no teeth?
A gummy bear.

What invention allows us to see through walls?
Windows.

DAUGHTER IS READING
THE DAD JOKES BOOK
BEFORE HER DAD
TO BE PREPARED
FOR THE WORST!

Why did the coach go to the bank?
To get his quarter back.

Why do nurses like red crayons?
Sometimes they have to draw blood.

What kind of jewelry do rabbits wear?
14 carrot gold.

Why can't the sailor learn the alphabet?
Because he kept getting lost at C.

I've ask so many people, what LGBTQ stand for.
So far no one has given me a straight answer

LITTLE GIRL LAUGHING AT HER DAD'S JOKE,
NOT KNOWING WHAT CONSEQUENCES
THIS WILL HAVE IN THE FUTURE

Why did the girl bring a ladder on the bus?
She wanted to go to high school.

What kind of music should you listen to while fishing
Something catchy

Why can't you trust a balloon?
It's full of hot air

How did the barber win the race?
He knew a shortcut.

What's more unbelievable than a talking dog?
A spelling bee.

WHY

**Why did the scarecrow become
a successful politician?**
Because he was outstanding in his field.

**What do you get when you cross a
snowman and a vampire?**
Frostbite

Where did the cat go after losing its tail?
The retail store

What do you call a moose with no name?
Anonymoose

Not sure if you have noticed, but I love bad puns.
That's just how eye roll

IMPRESS
Monsoon Publishing LLC

Email
info@monsoonpublishing.com

Website
www.monsoonpublishing.com

Facebook
www.facebook.com/monsoonpublishingusa

Etsy
www.etsy.com/shop/MonsoonPublishingUSA

Amazon USA Search
Monsoon Publishing

www.ingramcontent.com/pod-product-compliance
Lightning Source LLC
LaVergne TN
LVHW021309200726
843509LV00012B/1852